MW00909314

THE *Kennedy* COLLECTION

HOW I KNOW

THE *Kennedy* COLLECTION

HOW I KNOW

D. JAMES KENNEDY, PH.D.

Edited by Karen VanTil Gushta, Ph.D.

D. JAMES
KENNEDY
MINISTRIES

FORT LAUDERDALE, FL

THE KENNEDY COLLECTION
HOW I KNOW

By D. James Kennedy, Ph.D.
Edited by Karen VanTil Gushta, Ph.D.

All scripture quotations, unless otherwise indicated are taken from The Holy Bible, English Standard Version, copyright © 2001 by Crossway Bibles, a division of Good News Publishers. Used by permission. All rights reserved. Scripture quotations marked (NKJV) are taken from the New King James Version®. Copyright © 1982 by Thomas Nelson, Inc. Used by permission. All rights reserved.

ISBN: 978-1-929626-76-2

Jacket and Interior Design: Roark Creative, www.roarkcreative.com

Printed in the United States of America

Published by:

D. James Kennedy Ministries
P.O. Box 11786
Fort Lauderdale, FL 33339
1-800-988-7884
DJKM.org
letters@djkm.org

D. JAMES
KENNEDY
MINISTRIES

CONTENTS

These things I have written to you who believe in the name of the Son of God, that you may know that you have eternal life, and that you may continue to believe in the name of the Son of God.

— 1 John 5:13 NKJV

INTRODUCTION

P resident Ronald Reagan once said of his political opponents: "It's not that they are ignorant; they just know so many things that aren't so." Well, before we laugh too heartily at that, there are a great many things we think are true that are in fact not so.

For example, did you know that Napoleon Bonaparte was not short? He was actually slightly taller than the average French soldier. Did you know that Marie Antoinette never said: "Let them eat cake?" She was only nine years old when that phrase first appeared in the writings of Rousseau. Did you know that Albert Einstein did not fail a mathematics class? That popular misconception falls before the truth that Einstein mastered advanced calculus by age fifteen. How about the Great Chicago Fire of 1871? Did you know that Mrs. O'Leary's cow did not start that fire by kicking over a lantern? A newspaper reporter made up that little piece of fake news, thinking it sounded more colorful. And as we can see, not much has changed in journalism in nearly 150 years.

All of which raises an important question: How can we know that the things we believe are true? Or more generally how can we know anything with certainty?

In a day of falsified climate data, fabricated research, and fake news this is no small question. Yet, the answer is fairly straightforward. Everything we know comes to us in one of two ways—either by rationalization or revelation. You can either reason it out for yourself, or it can be revealed to you.

Christianity is a revealed religion. Both the light of creation and conscience reveal it to us. Prophets of old revealed it to us when they came saying: "*Thus says the Lord God of Israel.*" It came to us by the written Word of God—and it came to us when that living Word became flesh and dwelt among us. The apostle tells us why He came: "*And we know that the Son of God has come and has given us understanding, so that we may <u>know him </u>who is true*" (1 John 5:20).

By this we have confidence that the things we believe are true. It is to this task that Dr. Kennedy dedicates himself in the messages that follow, as he addresses the great question of our time: "How can I know?"

Frank Wright, Ph.D.
President and CEO
D. James Kennedy Ministries

CHAPTER 1

HOW I KNOW
THERE IS A GOD

The fool says in his heart, "There is no God."
They are corrupt, they do abominable deeds;
there is none who does good.

— Psalm 14:1

There is no more profound question that you can ask than this: Is there a God? Mortimer Adler, the famous scholar, educator, and editor of the *Great Books of Western Civilization,* in his *Great Ideas Syntopicon* (which is the topical index for the *Great Books),* says that almost every writer in Western civilization has written on the subject of God, with the exception of certain mathematicians and physicists. The chapter on God is the largest in these volumes. "The reason," he says, "is obvious. More consequences for thought and action follow the affirmation or denial of God than from answering any other basic question."

IS THERE A GOD?

Indeed, the entire tenor of our lives will be completely affected by the answer we give to the profound question: Is there a God? It has been asked for countless centuries, not only by adults, scholars, and educators, but also, even by children—and the latter have some interesting ways of asking that question. For example, this letter was sent to God.

Dear God,
Are you real? Some people don't believe it. If you are, you better do something quick.

Harriet Ann

Or this from a young but cautious skeptic:

Dear Mr. God,
How do you feel about people who don't believe
in you? Somebody else wants to know.

A friend,
Nell

Or from Charlene:

Dear God,
How did you know you were God?

Only a child would think of that.

Indeed, there are more implications for thought and
action generated by the question, "Is there a God?" than
any other question. Since the time of the Enlightenment,
with its assault on belief in God, a number of consequences
have followed. We live in what might be called, among
other things, "an age of atheism." Atheism has indeed
grown markedly in our time. Though 94 percent of
Americans profess belief in God, we have seen that atheist
societies are active and busily engaged in propagating
their views. The secular humanists are subtly inculcating
atheism in the students in our country's public school
system. Communism, now in over a third of the world,
also has done its best to promote atheistic belief.

Of course, when Nietzsche's "God is dead" philosophy became a reality in the lives of many people, something unexpected happened: man died also, because we have discovered that it is ineluctably true that when God dies, the significance of man ceases as well. If our beginning came out of nothing, and if our destiny is to go to nothing, then it is extremely difficult to prove that our brief existence here has any significance to it whatsoever.

Furthermore, from the atheistic perspective, man no longer has any purpose; there is no reason for our existence. Therefore, life becomes purposeless. It has been this discovery on many a college campus that has led a vast number of college students ending their lives prematurely.

DEATH OF MORALITY

We have also discovered that with the death of God goes the death of morality. Men have finally realized that you can't produce any valid ethical system without God. You may sit down and write up a set of ethics—but it will do no good, because nobody will pay any attention to it. It has no authority and it has no teeth in it. Who cares what you or I say people ought to do? You see, it is a problem of the authority that lies behind ethical systems that gives them their bite.

Recently, the president of Yale University, in a meeting

of university educators, professors, and presidents, made an apparently innocuous statement. It would seem to be as trite as "mom and apple pie"—not that moms are trite, but the statement is. He said that we need to have a revitalization of the intellectual and moral lives of our university students. Wouldn't you think people would just nod their heads and say, "Of course, that is desperately needed in our country today"? However, what was the result of that innocuous statement? It was met with boos and catcalls—from professors! Somebody stood up and said, "Whose morality are you going to impose upon them, professor? Yours?"

If God doesn't exist, the only morality we have is Dick's or Harry's or Susan's or Bill's or a committee that gets together and devises one! I have been asked why I thought I should impose my morality on somebody. I responded, "I'm sorry, sir, I never tried to impose my morality on anyone for the very simple reason that I don't have one. I don't have one because I never invented one. I have never, ever sat down and written up a set of ethics or morals for the human race or any portion of it to follow." Have you? Vast numbers of people who don't believe in God have!

I am quite happy to accept the morality God gave to us at Mount Sinai, which was further expanded in the Sermon on the Mount. I have none of my own. The question then is not whether morality is mine or someone else's, or whether it is God's or man's. With the death of God, we find the death of morality.

We have gotten rid of God in our schools, so now some schools have policemen in their halls . . . police dogs are in some of our high schools . . . and (here in Florida) we have metal detectors to keep the students from shooting the principal and the teachers—and a lot of other things that come with the death of God. The death of God brings about the ultimate demise of man.

So, is there a God? Let's consider what may seem to some to be an audacious subject: "How I Know There Is a God." In an age when many people feel you can't know anything; to say that I know there is a God, of all things, would seem to them to be utterly preposterous. I don't believe that it is. I think the Scripture very clearly tells us that we can know God: "*And this is eternal life, that they know you, the only true God, and Jesus Christ whom you have sent*" (John 17:3).

How do I know there is a God? Let me set forth several classic arguments for the existence of God, brought up-to-date in light of some modern scientific findings that certainly have an impact upon them.

THE COSMOLOGICAL ARGUMENT

One of the oldest arguments, going all the way back to Aristotle, is called the Cosmological Argument. ("Cosmological" simply means the study of the cosmos; the universe). The Cosmological Argument is basically an argument that says that for every effect there must be an adequate cause.

If we are looking for arguments or proofs for the existence of God, we don't have to look under a table or in a corner somewhere—all we have to do is look about us. The universe is the biggest thing there is, physically; and in itself, it is the greatest proof for the existence of God. This has been recognized from the very beginning of thinking men. The universe is the greatest and largest argument for God.

Notice: if the universe exists—and we all agree that it does—then there are only three explanations for it. One possibility is that it is eternal. There was a time when it was believed that this was so, but with modern scientific discoveries, it is no longer possible to believe that it is eternal. For the last 150 years, scientists have been scurrying around trying to avoid the plain implications of the modern laws they have discovered that clearly indicate that the universe is *not* eternal.

The great law, which is the most thoroughly documented of all the laws of science—the second law of thermo-dynamics, the law of entropy—says that everything is running down, everything is losing energy, everything is wearing out, everything is growing old. Therefore, it is very clear that if all of the universe were eternal, it would already have run down.

The universe and everything in it has a tendency to distribute its heat equally into all parts of the universe. The universe right now is trying to make every square foot of itself (the universe) the same temperature. The suns are getting cooler and the space is gradually receiving more and more energy. If you were to set a glass of hot water and a glass of cold water on a table and come back in a day, you would find that the water in both glasses would be the same temperature. Ultimately the entire universe would be the same tepid temperature if it continued long enough. There would be no freezing space; there would be no blazing sun. Yet, the universe has not run down; therefore, it is not eternal. Moreover, efforts to have an "oscillating" universe that would avoid this problem have all fallen afoul of recent scientific discoveries, which make it absolutely certain that the universe cannot be eternal.

The second possibility to consider is that if the universe is not eternal, maybe it is self-created—that is, it created itself out of nothing. However, this contradicts another scientific law, sometimes expressed in this way: *ex nihilo nihil fit* which means "out of nothing, nothing comes"; nothing is created from nothing. The universe cannot have created itself out of nothing. In fact, the concept flies in the face of the first law of thermodynamics, which says precisely that—nothing produces nothing.

A third possibility is that the universe was created by someone who is Himself eternal. That is the first statement of the Bible: "*In the beginning, God created the heavens and the earth*" (Genesis 1:1). That is the most scientific statement ever made about the origin of the universe. In light of all of the modern discoveries about the universe, it is becoming increasingly clear that the universe itself is a great argument for the existence of God.

Dr. Robert Jastrow, one of the leading space scientists in the world, head of the U.S. Institute for Space Studies and founder and head of the Goddard Space Institute for NASA, has said in his writings that modern scientific discoveries make it easier and easier for scientists to believe there is a God. In fact, they make it harder and harder for anyone to believe there is not.

WHERE DID LIFE COME FROM?

The second argument for God is the presence of life itself. From a cosmological perspective we have to ask, where did this life come from? This earth teems with life. It is a "sanctuary" in the universe, packed with living creatures. Where did they come from? It used to be held that life arose by spontaneous generation: flies and maggots coming into existence on putrid meat, frogs coming out of the slime of bogs. However, that was proved to be false by Louis Pasteur and Francesco Redi. So, the concept was abandoned; and since life was not coming into existence from non-life today, they retreated into the dim past. They said that, though life was not spontaneously coming into existence today, it did so millions of years ago—in fact, they like to say two billion years ago.

Very interestingly, discoveries that have taken place in the last decade or so have shown the impossibility of spontaneous generation of life from non-life. For example, consider protein, which not too many years ago was the most complex substance known to man. Protein molecules by the hundreds and thousands help make up a cell. They themselves are extremely complex and very different than the world Charles Darwin envisioned 125 or 130 years ago—he frequently talked about a "simple single cell." We know now that the complexity is such that Pierre Lecomte du Noüy, a French Nobel Prize-winning mathematician and one of the world's great experts in probability studies, said that the probabilities of even one protein molecule (one of the thousands of building blocks of the cell) coming into existence "would take 10^{234} billions of years to get the protein molecule [needed] for life. . . ."

Some of you, I am sure, do not appreciate what that means. Probability experts have said that if the probabilities of *anything* coming into existence are greater than

10 to the 50th power, it will never happen anywhere in the universe, regardless of how much time is involved. However, the probability to get simply one protein molecule is 10 to the 234th power–not 234 billion years, but 10 plus 234 zeroes billions of years.

Nevertheless, something even more complex than the proteins has been discovered: DNA. Drs. James Watson and Francis Crick discovered the key, the central brain of life in the nucleus of a cell, the DNA molecule. DNA exists in the form of a double-stranded helix, double circular stair-type of molecule, which is filled with the most complex of things. It is so complex that if you took each one of those DNA molecules out of your cells and stretched them out and linked them together, your body has enough DNA to reach from here to the sun and back 400 times! That is so complex that Francis Crick, co-discoverer of DNA and an atheist, said there is no possible way that even the DNA molecule could ever have arisen in this world by chance in even five billion years. He contends that the first protozoan must have been sent here by some advanced beings living in some other part of the galaxy. Where those beings came from, he didn't say. That is simply extending the shadow, an infinite regress in logic that will not work.

Meanwhile, Sir Fred Hoyle from Cambridge, one of the world's greatest mathematicians and astronomers, made a study of the possibility of a cell coming into existence anywhere in the entire history of the universe, and he discovered that the chances were zilch—ten to the 40 thousandth ($10^{40,000}$) power years to produce a cell. Ten with 40 thousand zeroes after it—it would take that many *years* to produce one cell.

The conclusion, said atheist Sir Fred Hoyle, "The only way life can possibly exist is that it was created by an infinite intelligence whom you may wish to call God." Therefore, atheist Fred Hoyle was forced to become a believer in God by the continuing advance of modern science.

THE TELEOLOGICAL ARGUMENT

Third, let me mention what is called the Teleological Argument. *Telos,* in Greek means "the end." This is the argument from ends or purposes or design. The argument from design says that all throughout the universe we see evidence of design. You look at a complex machine and conclude that it has a designer. That is the old watchmaker argument brought up to date.

The great astronomer Kepler had an acquaintance who was an atheist and with whom he had argued many a time. Kepler decided to construct a complex working model of the solar system that had the sun with the planets circling round it. It was a wonder to behold. One day his atheist friend came into his study and saw the great working model of the solar system. He was amazed! He was intrigued by its incredible complexity. He exclaimed, "How beautiful it is! Who made it?"

Kepler replied, "No one made it; it made itself."

His friend looked at him and said, "You don't expect me to believe that, do you?"

Kepler said, "No, I don't, but you believe that the real solar system, which is vastly more complex than this simple model, just made itself. That is even more palpably absurd."

In the same matter of design, consider the cell. There is no possibility that this just happened. When you stop to think that not only is a cell incredibly complex, but also it is more complex than any machine man has ever made. The largest super computer that exists on this planet today is a veritable toy compared to the enormous complexity of every one of the hundred trillion cells in your body. Yet, would anyone believe that the largest computer in the world just happened to make itself by chance? In fact, one scientist said that the cell is more complex than the most complex computer ever made by man, or the most complex machine that has ever even been dreamt of by man.

The incredible complexity of the eye gave Darwin, he said, a headache; and well it should have. Each human eye is composed of over 107 million cells, with 7 million cones (allowing the eye to see in full, living color) and 100-million rods and all the incredible complexities of this wonderful camera—the most perfect camera ever known to man. Darwin himself said, "that the eye with all its inimitable contrivances ... could have been formed by natural selection seems, I freely confess, absurd in the highest degree."

GOD'S LOVING CARE

Consider also the care that has been shown in the creation of our habitat. If the earth were 10 percent closer to the sun, we would burn up; if it were 10 percent further away, all life would freeze and die. If the moon were one-fifth closer to the earth, we would have 50-foot tidal waves covering most of the earth every day.

We live on an earth very similar to an apple. The inside of the earth, to the extent of an apple, is mostly lava. The hard part of the earth is as thin, comparatively, as the skin of an apple. We are kept from being incinerated by that lava by the thinnest of crusts. Above our heads are ultraviolet and other radiation that would also destroy us in but a few moments, but we are protected from them by the ozone layer and the atmosphere. God has indeed designed a wonderful habitat for man.

Water is one of the few liquids that expands when it freezes. If it contracted like most everything else, all of the lakes and rivers would freeze from the bottom up and all fish life would be killed.

The atmosphere is just thick enough to save us from countless millions of meteorites that burn up in it every day. All of this shows the care of a loving God who has cared for us.

One person wrote a poem to a doubter, which I think says it very well:

Oh you who could not put one star in motion,
Who could not build one mountain out of earth,
Or trace the pattern of a single snowflake,
Or understand the miracle of birth,
Presumptuous mortal who cannot alter the
    universe in any way,
Or fashion one small bud, release one raindrop, or
    toss one cloud into a sunny day.
Oh earthling who could never paint a sunset or
    cause one dawn to shine.
Oh puny man who cannot create a single miracle,
How dare you doubt the only One who can?

NOTED BELIEVERS

The American Atheist Society says that "Godism" is the result of ignorance and contributes to ignorance. They claim this in spite of the fact that the first 126 universities and colleges in this country were established by believers in God and Christ and to His glory. They claim this, in spite of the fact that among the most brilliant people upon this earth, the number who have believed in God is so vast that we could quote them from now until a week from Sunday and never run out! Just a few might be illustrative:

- The great philosopher Aristotle, with his gigantic intellect, who, it was said in his day, knew everything there was to know in the entire world about everything, said: "The beauty, order, and harmony of the universe is an expression of the will of God; the structure of the universe is the work of a great intelligence. . . ."

- Sir James Jeans, a modern astronomer said, "The more we examine the universe, the more it seems to be the single thought of a great mathematician."

- Albert Einstein, who, I think the most vicious critic would have to admit, was a man of some intellectual capacity, said, "I pity the man who says there isn't a Supreme Being . . . Everyone who is seriously involved in the pursuit of science becomes convinced that a spirit is manifest in the laws of the universe—a spirit vastly superior to that of man and one in the face of which we with our modest powers must feel humble."

- Socrates, who gave us the Socratic method of teaching, said: "There can be no happiness in life greater than communion with God, the Creator of the universe."

- The great physicist Michael Faraday said: "I bow before Him who is Lord of all."

- Pascal, the great French scientist, said, "The evidence of God's existence and his gift is more than compelling…"

- Thomas Edison said that his studies led him to the "inevitable conclusion that there is a Big Engineer who is mining this universe."

- Galileo said that "he would infer with certainty the existence of an intelligent Creator."

Statesmen have also expressed a belief in God.

- Ben Franklin, statesman and early American writer, stated: ". . .(T)he longer I live, the more convincing proofs I see of this truth, that God governs in the affairs of men."

• Statesmen like Sir William Gladstone, Prime Minister of England, and Queen Victoria, and many others, have also expressed a belief in God.

• Every one of the Presidents of the United States has been a believer in God. Indeed, is Godism the result of ignorance? Ask President Dwight D. Eisenhower who said: "It takes no brains to be an atheist. Any stupid person can deny the existence of a supernatural power . . ." (Did you hear that, Madalyn Murray O'Hair?)

We could go on and on and on through thousands upon thousands of comments of the greatest and wisest of men and women. Whether you are talking about authors or philosophers, or composers, or statesmen, or scientists, or whatever, there have been many numbers of them who have come to believe in God.

TRANSFORMATION OF THE SOUL

There is also the evidence of conversion—the transformation of the human soul, which is so monumental as to defy explanation.

- Thousands of pages have been written trying to explain away the conversion of the Apostle Paul alone. What transformed this man from the bitter and hostile critic and adversary of Christ into His most loyal devotee?

- What changed that volatile and vacillating fisherman, Peter, into the rock that gave great strength to the early Church?

- What changed Augustine, greatest intellect of the first thousand years of this age, from a profligate and dissolute philosopher into the great intellectual champion of Christianity?

- John Calvin, perhaps the greatest mind of the last thousand years, said, "I was suddenly converted unto God."

- Martin Luther, who changed the face of Europe through the Reformation, came face to face with the God who changed his life.

- John Bunyan, that sinful tinker of Bedford,

met the living God and was changed into a great pastor and author of *Pilgrim's Progress.*

• Or consider John Wesley and John Knox.

• Or more recently, C. S. Lewis, the atheist of Oxford and Cambridge, who wrote his testimony in his book *Surprised by Joy,* as he came face to face into the presence of that One whose existence he had always denied.

• Or perhaps the greatest literary man of the twentieth century—the Dostoevsky of our century—is no doubt the great Alexander Solzhenitsyn who met God while he was in the red belly of the dragon in the Gulag Archipelago.

• Or Billy Graham who, as a young, frivolous teenager, met the living God and Jesus Christ; his life was transformed, and through his ministry tens of millions of lives have been changed as well.

Who is going to explain these and hundreds and hundreds of millions of conversions of others who have led them across the widest oceans, up the highest mountains, through the densest jungles to proclaim the Gospel of Jesus Christ to cannibals, headhunters, and tribesmen of every sort. God has used them and their sacrifices to attest to the fact that there is a living God who changes human souls and makes them new creatures in Christ. But all of this will still be but theory until you come at last to that great experiment when, in the laboratory of your own soul, you meet with the ultimate proof.

How do I ultimately know there is a God? Because, my friends, one day 35 years ago I met Him face to face, person to person, in my own apartment, when he came to a young man who sought Him not and laid His hand upon my shoulder and turned me around. He transformed my heart, gave me totally different reasons for living, and for 35 years He has kept me going in a completely different way. I know there is a God because every day I meet Him and talk with Him. I know there is a God because He has changed my life.

He can change yours, too,

- when you come to see Him in all of His grace . . .

- when you come to see Him in the face of Jesus Christ hanging upon a Cross . . .

- when you see His wondrous love as He gave Himself for us in Christ . . .

31

- when you see His matchless grace . . .

- when He is willing to forgive you for all of your sins and to accept you just as you are and freely forgive you and gratuitously grant unto you the gift of everlasting life . . .

- when He is willing to give you the gift of Heaven, paid for by Him at infinite cost, by the sweat and blood and agony of the Cross, the wrath of His Father, the payment of Hell.

When you come to see a love like that, my friend, you will know there is a God—when you come to know that God as Lord and Savior of your heart.

᠊ᢀ

PRAYER: *Father, there are some reading this who do not know You. May your Spirit reach down and touch their lives right now. Open their blind eyes that they may see the face of Christ, the living God. May they surrender their lives to Him, repenting of their sins and inviting Him to take His place upon the throne of their hearts, placing their hopes of eternal life in His atoning death. I pray this in His most matchless name. Amen.*

CHAPTER 2

HOW I KNOW THE BIBLE IS GOD'S WORD

All scripture is given by inspiration of God, and is profitable for doctrine, for reproof, for correction, for instruction in righteousness.

— 2 TIMOTHY 3:16 NKJV

The Bible is the most astonishing and incredible book in the entire history of the human race, and Christians have always believed that it is the Word of God. This amazing book has been published in more editions . . . printed in more versions . . . translated into more languages . . . distributed in more copies . . . than any other book in the history of mankind—without even a close second. Well over nine billion copies of the Bible have been printed and distributed. That's almost two for every single person presently upon the face of the earth!

There are many people, however, right here in America who have no idea how remarkable and astonishing this book is. The Scriptural ignorance that exists in our country today is profound and lamentable.

But how do we know that the Bible is indeed God's Word? There are 26 other so-called scriptures, which are claimed by their followers to be words from God. So what proof is there that the Bible is indeed God's Word?

Charles Wesley, the famous hymn writer, said that the Scriptures obviously were either written by good men and angels; or by bad men and demons; or, thirdly, by God. Now, they could not have been merely written by good men or angels because over 2,600 times in the Old Testament alone, they claim they were written by God. Also, it is incredible that good men could lie about the same subject 2,600 times. How frequently we read, "Thus says the Lord . . . Thus says God Almighty . . . There came the Word of God unto the prophet saying. . . ."

Could the Scriptures have been written by bad men? Is it conceivable to suppose that bad men or demons authored a book that claims to lift mankind and which, in fact, historically, has done so to the highest level of morality and purity, which demands the most exacting standards of righteousness, and which proclaims upon all sinners a most dreadful doom? Would bad men write such a book, which declares that all liars shall have their part in the lake of fire? It is inconceivable, to say the least. Therefore, concluded Wesley, the only alternative is that the book was written by God.

But God Himself tells us how we may know whether a book has come from Him; whether a prophet has come from Him. He tells us: "*When a prophet speaks in the name of the Lord, if the word does not come to pass, that is a word that the Lord has not spoken;* (Deut. 18:21-22), because God is the only one who knows the future. He declares, *"I am God, and there is none like me, declaring the end from the beginning and from the ancient times things not yet done . . ."* (Isaiah 46:9-10).

As one historian says, "The future turns on too many slippery ball-bearings for any human being to be able to know it." The truthfulness of that statement is constantly seen in the ludicrous attempts by modern prophets, seers, and psychics who "proclaim the future" and who usually get little, if anything, right at all.

SPECIFIC DESCRIPTIVE PROPHECIES

None of the other so-called scriptures of the world contain specific predictive prophecies—only the Bible. The Old Testament alone contains well over 2,000 specific predictive prophecies that have already been fulfilled. There is no other book in the history of the world that contains anything vaguely resembling this. Here the entire future of the great cities that Israel had some sort of consort with is described. Here the future of nations is laid out before us so that any high school student with an encyclopedia can ascertain its truthfulness.

For example, there are over 100 specific predictive prophecies concerning the great city of Babylon, including such things as the fact that the wall of Babylon would be destroyed and never be built again; that the mighty city of Babylon would be destroyed and would never be inhabited again. Such prophecies were unheard of and such calamities were unknown when they were written, for every great city that had ever been destroyed had been built again on top of the ruins of its predecessor. But here are these bold and astounding assertions of the Scripture. These and over 100 more predictions about Babylon alone have already been fulfilled, and the test of time and the passing of centuries have failed to overthrow them.

The Scripture says that Babylon shall become pools

of water; that Babylon shall also become as a desert. Now, apparently those are contradictory prophecies and could not both come true. Yet travelers and explorers tell us that at some part of the year Babylon is as dry as the desert, and at other times the waters of the Euphrates overflow its banks and the land becomes filled with pools and lakes. And so, in an incredible way, the prophecy was fulfilled.

Concerning Jesus Christ, there are over 333 specific predictive prophecies that describe every detail of His life. Keep in mind that Nostradamus made a great reputation for himself, principally concerning one supposed prophecy regarding the rise of Hitler. He even got the name wrong—he calls him "Hisler." But he doesn't designate exactly where or when he would live.

Yet there are 333 prophecies concerning Jesus Christ that give us the exact date when He would come into the world (see Daniel 9); the exact place—Bethlehem Ephrathah (Micah 5:2); the incredible nature of His birth—that He would be born of a virgin (Isaiah 7:14). Furthermore, all of the details of His ministry and His career . . . His character . . . His betrayal for 30 pieces of silver . . . His crucifixion . . . the piercing of His hands and His feet . . . His burial in the grave of a rich man . . . His resurrection from the dead . . . His ascension into Heaven . . . His proclamation to the Gentiles—these and hundreds of other particulars are specifically set forth in the Old Testament prophecies.

There is *nothing in all of the literature* of mankind that even vaguely approaches this sort of thing.

THE UNITY OF THE SCRIPTURE

Another evidence of the divine authorship of the Scripture is the amazing unity of the book—something which most people would overlook. But, stop and think. The Bible is composed of 66 different chapters or books. These books were written by about 40 different authors, living on several different continents, and in numerous different nations—such as Israel, Babylon, Greece, Rome, Asia Minor, and, perhaps, Arabia. They were written in three different languages: Hebrew, Aramaic, and Greek. They were written by people who lived some 60 centuries apart! Yet, there is the same golden theme that runs through all of these books—the golden thread of the redemption of sinful man by the grace of God through faith in the shed blood of the Redeemer.

Now keep in mind that there was no publisher who commissioned the writing of such a book; there was no editor who gave forth a plan; there was no editorial committee that oversaw its development; there was never an outline spread about to the different authors. Yet, in spite of the fact that there is every sort of literature, including prose and poetry, history and law, biography and travel, genealogies, theologies, and philosophies, and all sorts of other forms of literature—nevertheless, all of these combine to provide an incredible unity from Genesis to Revelation.

Consider, for example, a painting. Suppose that 40 different artists were to paint a piece of a picture without having any idea what the others might be doing—or that others were doing anything at all. Yet, if someone were to collect these pieces and arrange them all upon a huge wall, and the result was a tremendous picture which delineated all of the features of Jesus Christ, it would be absolutely incredible!

Or suppose that 40 different sculptors, without any knowledge of what the others were doing, each decided to make a piece of sculpture. And yet when the pieces were glued together it was found to be a beautiful statue of Christ. That would be beyond our comprehension.

There is no other book in the entire world that has ever been made in this way. Having written a number of books, I know what publishers and editors and editorial committees do. None of this was involved. Yet, we have this incredible unity of a book, which testifies that the hand that made this book is divine.

THE INDESTRUCTIBILITY OF SCRIPTURE

Thirdly, we know the Bible is God's Word because of its indestructibility. You should realize that no other book in the history of mankind has ever endured such continued attack by so many, for so many ages. For 2,600 years, all of the powers of this world have combined to destroy this book and yet it still remains. The anvil stands: the hammers lie broken about it.

As one person said, it is somewhat like the Irishman's wall. One Irishman built a wall four feet high and five feet thick around his farm. Someone asked him why he made it so thick. He replied, "If anyone knocks it over, it will be higher than it was before." Now this doesn't prove that the Bible was written by an Irishman (as sad as that may seem for a Kennedy!), but it does show the remarkable hand of God that was involved.

Wicked King Manasseh of Judah, born in 697 B.C., was such a violent, ungodly pagan man that he determined to destroy all of the copies of the Mosaic Law because they denounced the kinds of activity in which he was involved—all manner of abominations, even including the sacrifice of children to the pagan god Molech. He succeeded in destroying all of the copies of the books of Moses—except somebody hid one copy in the wall of the Temple!

Twenty years after his death, his grandson Josiah ascended to the throne. He discovered that copy of the Law, which had almost been forgotten. He proclaimed that it should be read, and that all Israel should gather together to hear the reading of the Law of God. The result of this reading was a tremendous religious revival among the Israelites. Indeed, the "Irishman's wall" had been turned over and found to be taller than before!

During the Intertestamental period between Malachi and Matthew, Antiochus Epiphanes, that wicked Syrian tyrant, conquered Israel. He offered a pig on the altar of the Temple, murdered all of those who owned a Scripture and forbade their possession. Yet, this led to the Maccabean Revolt. No sooner was Antiochus in his grave than there was a great revival of interest in the Scripture and numerous copies were made.

In the New Testament era, in 303 A.D., Emperor Diocletian, one of the last great persecutors of the Church, saw that the Bible was the great source of the Christians' courage in opposing his paganism. He ordered the confiscation of all Christian property and the destruction and burning of all Scriptures. Only ten years passed before Diocletian was dead and Constantine the Great had arisen in his stead to sit upon the throne of Rome. He himself had come to trust in Christ as his Savior. He not only ordered the writing of many copies of the Scripture, but encouraged everyone in the Roman Empire to read the Bible of the Christians. Again, the "Irishman's wall" gets higher.

In the Middle Ages (Dark Ages) even the clergy placed the Bible on a list of banned books. The Synod of Toulouse forbade anyone from possessing a copy of the Scriptures.

Those, such as Tyndale, who tried to translate it into the vernacular of the people, were burned alive. Huss, who proclaimed that the Bible was the final authority, was burned alive. Wycliffe, who translated the Scripture into English, couldn't be burned alive because he died too soon; but his bones were exhumed and burned and his ashes scattered into the river. Yet, that river went out into the sea, symbolic of the fact that his Scriptures would spread to all of the nations of the world.

Bloody Mary ordered that anyone possessing a copy of the Bible would be burned to death. But five years after that edict, she was dead and gone. Queen Elizabeth ascended to the throne of England. During her time as queen, she ordered no less than 130 different editions of the Bible to be published—and the "Irishman's wall" kept getting bigger!

Voltaire, the famous French skeptic who so viciously attacked the Scriptures all of his life, prophesied that 100 years after his death the Bible would be gone and forgotten and might only be found by some antiquarian in some musty and dusty old bookshelf. Yet, immediately after his death, his printing press was used to print Bibles! His house in Geneva was bought by the Genevan Bible Society and used for the distribution of Scripture. Two hundred years after his death, on the very same day (Christmas Eve) a copy of a first edition of Voltaire's works sold for 11 cents and a copy of the Scriptures, the Codex Sinaiticus, sold for $500,000! So much for the "prophet" Voltaire!

In more recent times, higher critics have done their best to destroy the Scriptures from within. And yet never has an elephant labored longer to produce a mouse—because all of their efforts only seemed to confirm the historicity and truthfulness of the Bible.

CONFIRMATION BY ARCHAEOLOGY

Fourthly, we should note the confirmation of Scripture by archaeology. This is one of the wonders of our time. For the last 150 years, archaeologists have traversed the lands of the Bible; many times with hostile intent and with great animus toward the Scripture, attempting to disprove it. Yet every time they turned over their spades, it seemed they discovered another confirmation of the Scripture.

For example, there is the famous case of the Hittites. The Hittites, which are mentioned some 40 times in Genesis and other parts of the Old Testament, are described as a great empire. But there was not one single reference to the Hittite empire in all of secular literature, leading critics to believe that since it is described in the Bible and not in secular literature, then ergo!— obviously the Bible must be wrong. It is simply one of the mythological peoples of the dream world of the Bible, they said. Yet today, archaeology has uncovered the great Hittite empire so that we know vast details about it.

Or, take the case of Assyria. Did you know that 100 years ago, almost nobody outside of those who believed the Bible believed that Assyria ever existed? There was not one single secular reference to the great empire of Assyria. It was another one of the "mythological" empires of the Bible. Then a man went there and did some digging. He uncovered a brick that had on it the name of Sargon, whom the Bible says was a king of Nineveh, the capitol of Assyria. He sent it to scholars in Paris, who examined it and reached this profound conclusion: Since Nineveh was supposedly the capitol of Assyria, and Sargon was supposedly the king of this land, and since Assyria never existed, obviously—as any intelligent person can see—this is a fraud and a fake. But our intrepid discoverer had the temerity to go ahead and uncover the whole city of Nineveh, including the city's great library, which contained tens of thousands of cylinders and tablets giving the entire history of the great empire of Assyria, including the exploits of King Sargon.

Is there any high school student in the world today that doesn't know about Assyria? Where are the Biblical critics now? William F. Albright, famed archaeologist of Johns Hopkins University, has said that it can be stated that archaeology has substantially attested to the entire historicity of the Old Testament tradition.

Nelson Glueck, another famed archaeologist, said that it can be categorically stated that not one single archaeological discovery has ever controverted a Biblical text. So the Bible shows its divine origin by the fact that the more we learn about the people and the time that it describes, the more we see that it was in fact true.

THE TRANSFORMING POWER OF SCRIPTURE

Fifthly, let me mention the transforming power of the Scripture. The Bible says that it will transform nations and peoples that believe it.

The famous story, *Mutiny on the Bounty,* which was told in a book and a motion picture, was based on fact. Yet, the story I am going to tell you does not appear in the motion picture. After the sailors on His Majesty's Ship *Bounty* mutinied and went ashore on one of the South Sea Islands, a number of them decided to leave before the British came back and found them and hanged them. So they took some of the native women and sailed to another island. But soon they began fighting among themselves for the women and for the few possessions that they had. There were murders, and soon it seemed that the entire colony would destroy itself. Finally, one man discovered a Bible in one of the great casks that were brought from the ship. He began to read it and was transformed. He began to read it to others and soon the whole colony was changed.

Years later, His Majesty's forces discovered these renegades, these mutineers, living on this island. But they found that they had produced such a model society based upon the teachings of the Scriptures, that they dropped all charges against them.

Not only does the Bible transform societies, but it also provides for us many of the greatest things that make civilizations possible. It has provided for us literature and education. We have found that even literacy comes mostly from the Scriptures. It is easily seen that literate nations are nations where the Bible has gone. Where the Scriptures have not gone—or to the degree that they have not gone—there is found illiteracy to that same degree. We find that public education, republican forms of government, freedom from despotism—all of these things are part of the great heritage we have from the Scripture.

THE WORK OF THE HOLY SPIRIT

Lastly, let me say this. Ultimately, the divine authority of Scripture is experienced in the human heart, in the laboratory of the human soul, by personal and intimate experience with the Author of Scriptures who is the Holy Spirit. When the Holy Spirit comes to take up His residence in the human heart, people come to know that this indeed is the Word of the living God.

Well over 30 years ago, as a young man, I invited Jesus Christ to come into my life when I heard the Word of His glorious grace, and He changed my life. As a person who had no interest in the Scriptures, I suddenly found a hunger for it.

Many people are not interested in the Word of God. They are not interested in going to church. The reason is that they have never been changed by the Spirit of God. They do not know God. They are strangers and aliens to the Commonwealth of God, and they are yet in their sins. They are dead in their transgressions and sins; they are yet under condemnation; they are on their way to eternal death.

But my friends, if you have come to know Christ, then His Spirit has come into your life and He has given you a hungering and a thirsting for that Word.

These and many other evidences conclusively demonstrate the Scriptures are indeed the very Word of God. And if they are, then let me say this to you, its promises are true: promises of eternal paradise for all those who will trust in the grace of God as it is revealed in Jesus Christ, for all those who will invite Christ to be the Lord and Savior of their lives—to come in and cleanse them and renew them and make them His own.

But it also means this: the promises that the Scripture

makes of eternal perdition and damnation are equally true. There are many who are blithely and ignorantly going through this world—even as the Scripture describes them as dumb, brute beasts made to be taken and destroyed— who stagger off the precipice into the abyss without ever using the brain that God gave them to consider the evidences for the truthfulness of the Scripture.

Ah, the evidence is more than there. The problem is the sinfulness of the human heart of the person who doesn't want to know God, who doesn't want Christ in his life.

Where are you in all of this, my friend? Do you know the Savior that the Bible portrays and sets forth so graciously? Have you come to surrender your life to Him, or are you still living in rebellion . . . going your own way . . . doing your own thing . . . thinking your own thoughts . . . never giving a thought to the fact that it is God who created you . . . that it is God who gives you every breath that you draw . . . that it is God who offers you freely the gift of eternal life if you will simply trust in His grace . . . that it is God who is willing to forgive you for all your transgressions for which you should be smashed in His justice . . . that it is God before whom one day you will stand and have to give an account, and you will have to tell Him why it is that you never accepted His free offer of eternal life; why it is you have lived a rebellious life; why it is you have never surrendered your life to Jesus Christ.

My dear friend, "*Do not boast about tomorrow, for you do not know what a day may bring*" (Proverbs 27:1). This may be your last day upon this earth. God could not have done more. What more can He do for you than He has done—to give His Son and His promises and to establish them by irrefutable proofs, and yet some of you still, in the hardness of your own hearts, turn your back upon His offered love.

I urge you right now to repent of your sins. Open your heart and invite Him to come in. Surrender your life to Him while the day of grace still shines upon you.

❧

PRAYER: *Father, there are some reading this who desperately need Christ; whose hearts are hardened; who have turned their back upon You, and do not know that all too soon this life will be over and they will stand before a Holy God who will be outraged with them because of their sin. Then, for them there will be no hope; there will be no remedy, and there will be no end to eternity. O God, open their hearts; draw them unto You. Help them to pray right now, "Oh Christ, I am a sinner. I have gone astray. I have turned to my own way but now I repent, and I yield myself to You. Come into my heart. Cleanse me and renew me and make me Yours. In Your great name I pray. Amen."*

CHAPTER 3

HOW I KNOW JESUS IS GOD

Now when Jesus came into the district of Caesarea Philippi, he asked his disciples, "Who do people say that the Son of Man is?" And they said, "Some say John the Baptist, others say Elijah, and others Jeremiah or one of the prophets." He said to them, "But who do you say that I am?" Simon Peter replied, "You are the Christ, the Son of the living God." And Jesus answered him, "Blessed are you, Simon Bar-Jonah! For flesh and blood has not revealed this to you, but my Father who is in heaven."

— MATTHEW 16:13–17

Jesus Christ asked His disciples this question: *"Who do you say that I am?"* George Gallup answered it for us in a recent Gallup Poll entitled, "How America Sees Jesus." The poll revealed some interesting statistics: 81 percent of Americans profess themselves to be Christians; five percent profess themselves to be atheists; two percent claim to be Jews; and a few assorted others.[1] In addition, the poll showed 80 percent of Americans believe Jesus was the Son of God; however, only 42 percent believe that He was God among men. Now that is a tremendous discrepancy. I have repeatedly seen this in my own investigations, but here it is confirmed by a national survey.

WHAT IS MEANT BY "SON OF GOD"?

Who is Jesus Christ? Next to the question of whether or not there is a God; this is no doubt the most important question that can be urged upon the human mind. *"Who do you say that I am?"* Who is this one upon whom our hopes of Heaven depend? Who is Jesus? What is meant by the term "Son of God?"

It is interesting that in the motion picture titled *Oh,*

---

[1] Since Dr. Kennedy preached this sermon, these statistics have changed. The 2016 Gallup Poll of religious identification showed 72 percent identified as Christians, 7 percent identified as a non-Christian religion, and 18 percent identified as atheist, agnostic, or none (See: http://www.gallup.com/poll/200186/five-key-findings-religion.aspx)

God—that rather irreverent film—"God" is asked the question: "Is Jesus your son?" The cigar-smoking "God" replies, "Yes, he is my Son, and so is Buddha and so is Mohammed, etc."

What does it mean that Jesus is the Son of God"? Is that something different than the fact that He is God Himself? I have asked many people the question: "Who do you think Jesus Christ is?" I have received many answers. Some have said that He was just a man. Others have said that He was the Son of God. Probing their answer a bit to see if they understood what they were saying or whether it was merely a cliché, I responded, "Well, I am a son of God. Is He any different from me?" I assure you, that anyone who does not think Christ is different from me knows little about either of us, for if they did, they would know that there is an infinite gulf between us.

Who is this Jesus of Nazareth? What does it mean that He called Himself "the Son of God"? Now He frequently called Himself "the Son of Man." That is a messianic title taken from the Old Testament book of Daniel. But what did He mean by "the Son of God?" The Jews had no difficulty understanding it, whereas today millions of Americans seem quite perplexed and confused. When He said He was the Son of God, they became so enraged that they took up stones to stone Him. When He asked why they stoned Him—for what good works—they said it was not for any good work but rather *"because you, being a man, make yourself God"* (John 10:33), or paraphrased: "By calling God your Father, you are making yourself equal with God," and the Jews understood well what that meant.

During a conversation with a gentleman who thought that Jesus was just a man like anyone else, I said, "I think I have some startling and astonishing news for you. According to the Bible and the historic Christian Faith, Jesus of Nazareth was and IS the infinite, eternal Creator of the universe, the Almighty God." Instantly, his eyes filled with tears and he said to me, "I have never heard that before, and yet I have always thought that is the way it ought to be."

My friends, that is precisely the way it *is*! Jesus Christ *is* God—not a mere created being. The Trinity does not consist of the Father, the Holy Spirit, and the creature, but of God the Father, God the Holy Spirit, and God the Son. The fact that Jesus Christ is God incarnate— God in human flesh—is the most basic, most important, most distinctive teaching of the Christian faith. Only Jesus claimed to be divine, and only Christianity claims its Founder is divine. Moses made no such claim, nor did Buddha, nor did Muhammad, nor did Lao-Tse, nor did Confucius, nor did any other religious teacher. Only Jesus made that claim. This caused chaos among the Jews of Israel.

C.S. Lewis, the great scholar from Oxford and Cambridge, made an interesting comment about Jesus' claim to be God. He said: "Then comes the real shock. Among these Jews there suddenly turns up a man who goes about talking as if he was God. He claims to forgive sins. He says He always existed. He says He is coming to judge the world at the end of time."

It is also interesting that many people today think that the essence of Christianity is the teaching of Jesus. That is not so. The teaching of Jesus is very, very secondary to Christianity. In fact, you might be surprised to know that if you read the epistles of the Apostle Paul, which make up most of the New Testament, there is almost nothing whatsoever said about the teachings of Jesus. Not one of His parables is mentioned. In fact, throughout the rest of the New Testament there is little reference to the teachings of Jesus.

In The Apostles' Creed, that most universally-held Christian creed, there is no reference to the teachings of Jesus; there is no reference to the example of Jesus. In fact, the creed states: "[He was] born of the Virgin Mary, suffered under Pontius Pilate, was crucified, dead, and buried . . ." There are only two days in Jesus' life that are mentioned: the day of His birth and the day of His death, because, you see, Christianity centers not in the teachings of Jesus, but in the person of Jesus as the Incarnate God who came into this world to take upon

Himself our guilt and to die in our place.

Those of us in the ministry are repeatedly told in seminary that we are not to preach ourselves and that a very significant flaw in any minister's preaching is the continual preaching of self. That is considered to be totally out of place in the pulpit. Yet Jesus Christ, the Master Preacher, the Great Exemplar, constantly preached about Himself: *"I am the Good Shepherd . . . I am the Way . . . I am the Truth . . . I am the Light . . . I am the Door."* I, I, I! Christ was always preaching Himself because it is in the person of Christ that our hope of salvation is to be found.

WAS JESUS A GOOD MAN?

Many people say that Jesus was a good man. I want to say categorically, that is a lie! Jesus Christ was not a good man! Do you remember the account of when somebody came to Him and said, "*Good Master,*" and he replied, in effect, "Stop right there," or an old English equivalent, "*Why do you call me good?*" Jesus had just gotten through teaching that all men were sinful. Then someone comes and calls Him "good." Jesus said, "*Why do you call me good? No one is good except God alone.*" (Luke 18:19).

So you see, He hung him up on the horns of a dilemma! If Jesus were merely a man, He was not good, for He had just gotten through teaching that all men were sinful. If Jesus were good, then He was God, because He had just gotten through teaching that there is only one who is good and that is God. If Jesus is good, He is God; if Jesus is not God, He is not good.

Again, C.S. Lewis puts this in a very memorable language for us. He said:

I am trying here to prevent anyone saying the really foolish thing that people often say about Him: "I'm ready to accept Jesus as a great moral teacher, but I don't accept His claim to be God." That is the one thing we must not say. A man who was really a man and said the sort of things Jesus said would not be a great moral teacher. He would either be a lunatic—on a level with the man who says he is a poached egg—or he would be the Devil of Hell. You must make your choice. Either this man was, and is, the son of God: or else a madman—or something worse. You can shut Him up for a fool, you can spit at Him and kill Him as a demon, or you can fall at His feet and call Him Lord and God, but let us not come up with any patronizing nonsense about His being a great human teacher. He has not left that open to us. He did not intend to.

Jesus was either God, or He was not a good man. He said that He was the only way to Heaven; that all who trusted in Him would be everlastingly saved. If anybody denied Him, he would be denied before the Father and would be shut out from Paradise. Based upon those teachings, countless millions of people suffered the agonies of the arena. They were covered with tar and lighted as torches for Nero's garden. They were placed in sacks with vipers. They were thrown to the lions. They were killed in a thousand different ways that the depravity of man could invent.

If Jesus was not all that He claimed, then He was a great demon, or the arch deceiver of all times. But the Christian Church, in all of its branches—all historic Christian denominations (and I say it that way merely to exclude the cults)—have held that Jesus Christ was 100 percent divine and 100 percent human. He was God and He was a man. He was the *theanthropos,* the God-man. All churches—whether Presbyterian or Orthodox, or any other, have all held that belief—except for the cults. (One of the sure signs of a cult is the denial that Jesus Christ is truly God.)

WHAT DO THE HISTORIC CREEDS SAY?

Let us just back that up with what the great creeds of the Church have said.

- The leaders of the Church from all over the inhabited world came together at the Council of Nicaea in 325, the first and greatest of the ecumenical councils. After many months, they wrote this statement in the Nicene Creed, which says: "We believe . . . in one Lord Jesus Christ, the Son of God, begotten of the Father as only begotten, that is, from the essence [reality] of the Father, God from God, light from Light, true God from True God, begotten not created."

- The Council of Chalcedon (451) stated: ". . . we unite in teaching all men to confess the one and only Son, our Lord Jesus Christ. This selfsame one is perfect both in deity and in humanness . . ."

- The Augsburg Confession of the Lutheran Church says: ". . . God the Son became man, born of the Virgin Mary, and that the two natures, divine and human, are so inseparably united in one person that there is one Christ, true God and true man . . ."

- The 39 Articles of the Church of England, the doctrine of the Episcopal Church, states:

"The Son, which is the Word of the Father, begotten from everlasting of the Father, the very [*very* means 'true'] and eternal God, and of one substance with the Father, took Man's nature in the womb of the blessed Virgin, of her substance: so that two whole and perfect natures, that is to say, the Godhead and Manhood, were joined together in one Person, never to be divided. . . ."

- The Westminster Confession of Faith, which contains the doctrinal statement of the entire Presbyterian world, says: "The Son of God, the second Person in the Trinity, being very and eternal God, of one substance, and equal with the Father did, when the fullness of time was come, take upon Him man's nature. . . ."

So it is true that throughout history, all historic branches of the Christian Church have proclaimed that Jesus Christ is God, the Eternal Creator of the universe.

WHAT DOES THE BIBLE SAY?

So now you ask: What does the Bible say, for that is our ultimate and final authority. Let me share with you some of the scriptural teachings, some of which you may have noticed before. I hope that there will be some unusual evidence, as well as some of the more common.

In Matthew 1:23, we read: "*Behold, the virgin shall conceive and bear a son, and they shall call his name Immanuel (which means, God with us).* In the very naming of the babe, He was God with us—God in human form.

In the first chapter of the most popular of all the Gospels, the Gospel of John, we read: "*In the beginning was the Word, and the Word was with God* [the Father], *and the Word was God . . . All things were made through him, and without him was not any thing made that was made . . . And the Word became flesh and dwelt among us . . .*" (John 1:1,3, 14). He said, "*Before Abraham was, I am*" (John 8:58). In Colossians, we read: "*For in him the whole fullness of deity dwells bodily*" (Colossians 2:9).

After Christ was raised from the dead and showed doubter Thomas His pierced hands and side, Thomas fell at His feet and said, "*My Lord and my God!*" (John 20:28). He is called ". . . *our great God and Savior Jesus Christ*" (Titus 2:13). Even the Father, Himself, after He has been speaking about the angels, speaks about the Son and this is what He says: "*Your throne, O God, is forever and ever*" (Hebrews 1:8). Speaking of Jesus Christ, the Scripture says: "*He is the true God and eternal life*" (1 John 5:20).

Therefore, we see that the Scriptures very clearly

teach that Jesus is God. In Isaiah 9:6, we read: *"For to us a child is born, to us a son is given; and the government shall be upon his shoulder, and his name shall be called Wonderful Counselor, Mighty God, Everlasting Father, Prince of Peace."*

Is the Father eternal? Out of Bethlehem, we are told there is to come that One *"whose coming forth is from of old, from ancient days"* (Micah 5:2). The Babe from Bethlehem is one who was eternally old when He was born.

Some other, perhaps less widely understood, evidences are found in the New Testament where all the attributes of deity are ascribed to Jesus Christ.

Is the Father Omnipresent? Jesus said, *"For where two or three are gathered in my name, there am I among them"* (Matthew 18:20). Not "will I be" but "am I." Every day of the week there are countless millions of groups meeting in the name of Jesus Christ, and in every one of those, Jesus is there demonstrating His omnipresence— one of the attributes of deity.

Is the Father Immutable? [unchangeable] Another one of the great attributes of deity. The Scripture says: *"Jesus Christ is the same yesterday and today and forever"* (Hebrews 13:8).

Is the Father Almighty? Creation demands omnipotence. The Bible says, *"All things were made through him, and without him was not any thing made that was made"*

(John 1:3). Not only did He create all things, but also He upholds them by the word of His power, "*and in him all things hold together*" (Colossians 1:17).

Is the Father himself incomprehensible, while comprehending all things? The Bible says of Christ: "*Lord, You know everything*" (John 21:17). "*No one knows the Son except the Father, and no one knows the Father except the Son*" (Matthew 11:27). "He who knows the Father is omniscient; he who is known only by the Father is incomprehensible" said Bickersteth.

Is the Father the Creator, Preserver, and Governor of all things in heaven and earth? So also is Jesus Christ.

Is the Father the Searcher of hearts? So also is Christ who says, "*I am he who searches mind and heart*" (Revelation 2:23).

Is the Father the Most High Judge of all? The Scripture says that all judgment is given into the hands of the Son. "*For we must all appear before the judgment seat of Christ*" (2 Cor. 5:10).

Therefore, we see that all the attributes of deity are ascribed to Jesus Christ except one; and that is the attribute of "invisibility." Of course, the reason for that is that Jesus Christ came to manifest the Father and make Him plain so that in Him we may see the image of the eternal God.

PROPHECIES FROM THE OLD TESTAMENT

There is other interesting evidence that most people have probably never seen: the repeated Scriptures in the Old Testament, which are prophecies of the coming Christ, that are fulfilled in the New Testament by Jesus—but in the Old Testament they are referring to Jehovah.

For example, in Isaiah 40:3 we read: "*A voice cries: 'In the wilderness prepare the way of the LORD* [Jehovah]; *make straight in the desert a highway for our God.'*"

John the Baptist attributed the very same title to Jesus when he said in Matthew 3:3: "For this is he who was spoken of by the prophet Isaiah when he said, 'The voice of one crying in the wilderness: "Prepare the way of the Lord; make his paths straight."'"

The biblical evidence for the deity of Christ is so voluminous that I do not have time to present to you even one-tenth of the evidence that is there. Another fascinating prophecy is found in Zechariah 12:10 where we read: "*And I* [Jehovah] *will pour out on the house of David . . . a spirit of grace . . . so that, when they look on me, on him whom they have pierced. . . .*"

In the New Testament we read: "*And again another Scripture says, 'They will look on him whom they have pierced.'*" In the New Testament, this is referring to Christ, but in the Old Testament it is Jehovah whom they shall look upon and whom they have pierced.

Who is Jehovah? Jehovah is the triune God. The Father is Jehovah; the Son is Jehovah; the Holy Spirit is Jehovah—the great "I Am."

Another evidence often missed is the fact that the Bible repeatedly says that we are to worship God only, and that no mere creature is ever to be worshipped. The angel, you will recall, jerked John to his feet and said that he was not to worship an angel, for he was a servant like unto him, but to worship God; that to worship any creature, by definition, is blasphemy.

Yet, in the Scripture we find that Jesus Christ, repeatedly, over and over again, received and even blessed the worship of men. We are told that He was worshipped by the Magi; He was worshipped by the leper; He was worshipped by the ruler; He was worshipped by the disciples; He was worshipped by the women and the disciples after the Resurrection. He was worshipped over and over again. If Jesus were merely a creature something less than God—He would have been receiving and blessing the blasphemy of men. When Thomas fell before Him [Jesus] and said, "*My Lord and my God*," Jesus did not rebuke him.

JESUS CHRIST IS GOD

Ah, my friends, Jesus is God, for if He were not God, He could not be our Savior. The Scripture makes it very plain that no mere man can redeem his brother. No mere man could pay the penalty for all the sins of the world. It took an infinite person, the God-man, to do that.

No mere man could hear the prayers of His people or answer them. Right this day there are hundreds of millions of people lifting their hearts and voices in prayer to Jesus Christ, in countless hundreds and hundreds of languages. How does He understand all of those prayers? If, indeed, He had taken a quick course in all the languages of the world and mastered each one, how does He hear them—millions at one time? He could not hear our prayers, much less answer them, if He were not God.

The great pulpiteer Alexander Whyte of Scotland said, "The longer I live, the firmer is my faith rooted in the godhead of my Redeemer. No one short of the Son of God could meet my case. I must have one who is able to save to the utmost."

Yes, my friends, Jesus Christ is God. Even the brilliant Napoleon Bonaparte, who in his days of exile gave himself to studying the Scripture, concluded: "I know men; and I tell you that Jesus Christ is not a man. Superficial minds see a resemblance between Christ and the founders of empires and the gods of other religions. That resemblance does not exist."

As the skeptic and writer E.A. Rowell, who was an infidel and an atheist (and grew up in such a home), said:

I was reared as an infidel. My parents and other immediate relatives were proud of their unbelief. I was nourished on the vaunting skeptics of the ages.

But I observed the futile amazement with which every skeptic from Celsus to Wells stood around the cradle of the Christ. I wondered why this helpless Babe was thrust into the world at a time when Roman greed, Jewish hate, and Greek subtlety could combine to crush Him. Yet, this most powerful, devastating combination ever known in history served to advance the cause of the Infant who was born in a stable. . . .

No unbeliever could tell me why His words are as charged with power today as they were nineteen hundred years ago. Nor could scoffers explain how those pierced hands pulled human monsters with gnarled souls out of a hell of iniquity and overnight transformed them into steadfast, glorious heroes who died in torturing flames, that others might know the love and mighty power of the Christ who had given peace to their souls. . . .

Nor could any scoffer explain, as Jesus Himself so daringly foretold why . . . His words are piercing the densest forest, scaling the highest mountains, crossing the deepest seas and the widest deserts, making converts in every nation, kindred, tongue, and people on earth.

No doubter could tell me how this isolated Jew could utter words at once so simple that a child can understand them and so deep that the greatest thinkers cannot plumb their shining depths. The life, the words, the character of this strange man are the enigma of history. Any naturalist's explanation makes Him a more puzzling paradox, a fathomless mystery.

However, I learned that the paradox was plain and the mystery solved when I accepted Him for what He claimed to be—the Son of God, come from heaven a Saviour of men, but above all, my own Saviour. I learned to thrill at the angel's words: "Behold . . . unto you is born this day . . . a Saviour, which is Christ the Lord." Now I have learned the great truth that:

"Though Christ a thousand times in Bethlehem be born,

If He's not born in thee, thy soul is forlorn."

WHO DO YOU SAY JESUS IS?

My friend, who do you say Jesus is? Can you say with Thomas, "*My Lord and my God*"? Have you come to know Him as your Divine Redeemer? He took upon

Himself at Calvary all of the guilt of all of our sins and suffered there at the hands of His own beloved Father the wrath that sin deserves, that you and I may be spared and may be taken to Paradise.

If you would ever live at the address which is God's, it will only be when you receive Him who is the Way, the Truth, and the Light, and without whom no man will enter into Heaven.

Who do *you* say that Jesus is?

PRAYER: *Father, help us to know that this is no mere historical or theological or philosophical question, but the most important question that any of us shall ever answer. One day we shall hear it from the lips of Christ Himself, in that day when every knee shall bow and every tongue shall confess that Jesus Christ is Lord, Jehovah. O God, may it be now while the day of grace still shines upon us, that we receive and accept Him as such, saying, "Lord Jesus Christ, Divine Redeemer, come. Wash me from my sins. Live in my heart. Transform my life and make me Yours. In Your most glorious and holy name. Amen."*

CHAPTER 4

HOW I KNOW CHRIST ROSE FROM THE DEAD

He presented himself alive to them after his suffering by many proofs, appearing to them during forty days and speaking about the kingdom of God.

— ACTS 1:3

The adherents of most of the major religions of the world can take their friends—if they happen to be traveling to the right spot—to a certain place and say with some (I believe misguided) pride, "Here is the grave of our great founder." This, Christians cannot do. We cannot say, "Here lies the body of the great founder of the Christian religion"—because the tomb is empty, and Jesus is not there; He has risen from the dead.

As we consider the subject "How I Know Christ Rose from the Dead," I would like to begin by presenting three reasons why it is one of the most important things in this world that we can ever know.

First, it is important because the resurrection of Christ is the foundation of our faith. With the Resurrection stands or falls the Christian religion. As Paul said, *"And if Christ has not been raised your faith is futile and you are still in your sins. . . . we are of all people most to be pitied"* (1 Corinthians 15:17, 19b).

Second, it is the Resurrection to which we can repair in times of doubt and trial. When it may seem that other things are going wrong and questions come to our mind, we can always go to the Resurrection. We can flee to that great Gibraltar of our faith and find place for our souls in the certainty of our salvation, resting upon the many infallible proofs that Christ has given of His resurrection life.

Third, the Resurrection is the most powerful weapon

in the arsenal of the Christian soldier. Those who would be effective witnesses for Christ need to realize that the Resurrection is the unassailable fortress of Christianity. All of the efforts of all of the skeptics down through the centuries have utterly failed to even put a dent in it.

To give you some idea of how solid and certain is the evidence of the Resurrection, let me give you my conclusion first. Many people believe that Christianity is based upon legends or myths or uncertainties—things that we really don't know about; that "wish" is really father of the thought, and all these disappear in the mists of time, and there is no real solid evidence for Christianity at all. They could not possibly be more mistaken. The number of testimonies from historians and legal scholars is so innumerable that it would take the rest of this message just to quote them.

So I'll limit myself to the testimony of Professor Thomas Arnold. He is author of the famous three-volume *History of Rome.* He was appointed to the chair of modern history at Oxford, the most prestigious institution of higher learning in the world—indeed a tremendous honor. This great historian and scholar said this: "I have been used for many years to study the histories of other times, and to examine and weigh the evidence of those who have written about them, and I know of no one fact in the history of mankind which is proved by better and fuller evidence of every sort, to the understanding of a fair inquirer, than the great sign which God has given to us that Christ died and rose again from the dead."

My friends, if the Resurrection of Christ be not true, then we don't know anything about anything in all of the history of the world, because this is the best proved single fact of all.

Let me list a few of the many evidences for the Resurrection—some that you may never have thought of before. I am going to limit myself to only four, and then I will show you that the four classical, naturalistic explanations for the Resurrection—the four great attempts that have been made to explain away the Resurrection—can be and have been totally demolished by just a few of the evidences for the Resurrection.

YOU ARE HERE

The first evidence for the Resurrection is: *You!* That you are here as a part of the Church of Jesus Christ is a great evidence for the Resurrection of Jesus Christ. One billion, six hundred million people in the world today are part of that Church. It is the largest institution that exists or has ever existed on planet earth. Somebody has well said that the Grand Canyon wasn't created by an Indian dragging a stick. Likewise, the largest institution in the world wasn't created by the figment of somebody's imagination.

How *did* it come about? It is interesting that skeptics are agreed as to how it came about. On what are they agreed? They are agreed that about 30 A.D. in the city of Jerusalem, the apostles of Jesus of Nazareth began to preach that He had been raised from the dead. That message of the resurrection of Jesus from the dead spread all over Israel and all over the Near East and all over the Roman Empire and transformed the world.

Even H. G. Wells, a notorious skeptical critic, makes it very clear in his volume, *The Outline of History,* that after Christ died it was the preaching of the apostles that Jesus had been raised from the dead that gave birth to the Church. Now, Wells doesn't believe that they were correct in what they were saying (and we shall look into that in a moment), but I am simply trying to impress upon you that the Church of Jesus Christ, this "Grand Canyon" of institutions—was created by the preaching of the resurrection from the dead. In fact, the apostles were chosen as those who were eye witnesses to the resurrected Christ. Now, every effect must have an adequate cause to explain it.

THE FIRST DAY OF THE WEEK

A second evidence for the Resurrection is simply this: You are here today on Sunday and not Saturday. I am speaking of the tremendous change that took place in the day of the Sabbath. The first century Jews were fanatical Sabbatarians. They would stone a person to death for carrying a stick on the Sabbath. On several occasions they tried to kill Jesus for healing someone on the Sabbath.

The Early Church was made up almost entirely of Jews. How is it that these fanatical Sabbatarians were willing to abandon their century-old belief in the seventh-day Sabbath and begin to worship and rest and glorify God and have all of their church activities on the first day of the week and not on the seventh? There is only one explanation. It is given by the apostles themselves and their followers: because on the first day of the week, Jesus Christ rose from the dead. So, here we have this tremendous institution of the Christian Sabbath as a second evidence of the Resurrection.

The seventh-day Sabbath was given as a memorial, for on the seventh day the Lord rested from the creation of the heavens and the earth—the physical universe. The first-day Sabbath is a memorial of the creation of a new heaven and a new earth—of the Kingdom of God, which was ushered in by the resurrection of Christ from the dead.

THE EMPTY TOMB

The third evidence I would like to set before you is the fact of the empty tomb. Here is a rock upon which may be dashed to pieces all manner of doubts. Let me say that the entire testimony of antiquity is clear that the tomb of Jesus Christ was empty. It was never suggested by anyone at that time that the tomb was not empty.

In fact, the explanation that the priests told the soldiers to give for what had happened was that the disciples stole the body. None of them ever tried to refute the preaching of the Christians by saying, "What do you mean, He has risen from the dead? Why, He's still there. I just went out at my lunch break and checked the tomb. The seal is not broken. He is still entombed."

The tomb was empty and that fact, as you will see shortly, destroys and demolishes many a theory that has been brought up as to what happened to Jesus in attempts to deny the reality of the Resurrection.

POST-RESURRECTION APPEARANCES

The fourth evidence I would mention is the post-Resurrection appearances of Jesus. At least ten times Jesus appeared after the Resurrection and before His Ascension. Afterward, He appeared again to Paul on the road to Damascus and to John on the island of Patmos. But in the 40 days before He was taken up, He made numerous appearances to one or to two or to three or to eight or to eleven or to 500 people at one time. For about six weeks He appeared in the morning, at noon, at night, inside, outside, at breakfast, at dinner—at various times He met with them and they saw Him.

As a result of these appearances, the disciples were transformed. Their lives were totally revolutionized. But we need to remember what the state of the apostolic band was after the death of Jesus. They were totally demoralized. They were totally dejected. They were filled with fear. They locked themselves in an upper room for fear of the Jews. Simon Peter said, *"I am going fishing"* (John 21:3). They were about to go back to their homes, to disperse and give up the whole thing. The two disciples on the road to Emmaus said, *"We had hoped that he was the one to redeem Israel"* (Luke 24:21). But their hopes were dashed. The whole thing had collapsed. It was all a shambles. It was over, *fine,* kaput! He was dead and buried—the end!

Then, suddenly, apparently without any natural explanation, this group of frightened "little rabbits" turned into bold proclaimers of the resurrected Christ, who could stand before the Sanhedrin and declare unto them, *"Let it be known to all of you ... that by the name of Jesus Christ of Nazareth, whom you crucified, whom God raised from the dead—by him this man is standing before you well"* (Acts 4:10).

By the way, you should remember that Jesus did not appear merely to believers, as is often said. Jesus appeared to non-believers as well. He appeared to James, His half-brother, who with the rest of His half-brothers was totally contemptuous of His claims during His lifetime. They had wanted to bring Him home and hide Him away because they thought He was disgracing the family name. They mocked Him in His pretensions. And yet James, to whom the Bible declares Jesus individually appeared, became the great apostle of the church at Jerusalem, the leader of that church, and he was subsequently martyred for his faith. Jesus also appeared to Paul, who could not have been a stauncher unbeliever. He was a persecutor of the Church. He traveled as far away as to Damascus to ferret out Christians and to bring them back in chains for trial and execution in Jerusalem. However, Jesus appeared to both of these unbelievers and transformed them into the most heroic soldiers of the Cross of Christ.

Not only were these people transformed, but the ultimate proof of their sincerity was given when they shed their blood for what they believed. All of the apostles, except for John who was banished by Nero to the island of Patmos, gave their lives in martyrs' deaths, many of them dying in the most horrible ways—being crucified upside down, and tortured in every conceivable way. Yet they never denied their faith.

Let us consider just these four simple evidences for the Resurrection and the four naturalistic explanations that have been given in denial of the resurrection. If a person rejects Christ, he must in some way explain what happened: how the Church came about; how the Sabbath was changed; how the apostles were transformed; and why they gave their lives as martyrs.

THE FRAUD THEORY

The first effort to explain and deny Jesus' resurrection from the dead is known as the "fraud theory." That was the official view of the Sanhedrin. The priests gave large sums of money to the guards to say, *"His disciples came by night and stole him away while we were asleep"* (Matt. 28:13). The idea that while they slept, the disciples came and stole the body of Jesus, and now they were pretending that He had risen from the dead, is a very interesting theory. There are a few problems with it, however, to say the least. For example, in the first place, the disciples were anything but a group of people who were ready to do such a thing. Rather, they were ready to hide and cringe and flee and go home and get under the bed—not do something as bold as trying to overcome the Roman guards.

There is no question of the fact the guards were *not* asleep. No one said they were. The priests told them to say it of themselves, which was absurd. Here were sixteen of the most completely armed and disciplined Roman soldiers imaginable. To go to sleep on guard duty would result in being crucified upside down or to being burned alive in their own clothes. There was no way that any one of them would have been sleeping on guard duty.

In fact, if they had been asleep, that would have been quite interesting. Can you imagine their testimony in a courtroom: "Your Honor, while we were asleep, the disciples came and stole the body"? No one has ever been known to give testimony of what happened while he was asleep. If they were asleep, they certainly didn't know that the disciples were the ones that stole the body—if the body had been stolen.

But that was the fraud theory: a conspiracy among the disciples—a "Passover Plot," as it has been called.

Chuck Colson had an interesting insight into the possibility of this happening. Colson was the chief counsel to President Nixon. He was involved in the Watergate cover-up, and he went to prison for a brief period of time because of it. Colson said he has often been asked by reporters, especially on the anniversaries of Watergate: "What is the chief lesson you learned from Watergate?" He said he has often wanted to say to them that the chief lesson he learned from Watergate was that Jesus Christ must have risen from the dead. But he knew these secular reporters would think he had lost his mind so he hadn't said it. You might ask, "Why was that?"

Here were ten carefully selected, highly educated men around the very seat of power of the President of the United States who were involved in a fraud, a conspiracy, a cover-up. (Such as has been claimed here for Jesus.) Now, none of these men's lives was ever even conceivably threatened. Not one of them was facing the electric chair. They might have gotten a couple of year's prison sentence at the very worst. Yet these highly skilled lawyers were not able to contain this conspiracy for more than just a couple of weeks. In little more than two weeks the whole conspiracy unraveled!

John Dean was the first to make his way to the special prosecutor and, pleading for immunity, confess to the whole thing. Then another and another and another. None of them, said Colson, was doing it for any exalted patriotic or constitutional reason. They all were doing it, as they admitted, for one reason: to save their own skins.

Now, in the case of the Resurrection, these disciples were facing scourging and crucifixion—the most horrible form of death. I believe Dr. Principal Hill has put it most succinctly. He said that if you believe the testimony of the apostles that Christ was raised from the dead, then you can give the most natural account of every part of their conduct, of their conversion, of their steadfastness, of their heroism. He said, "But if, notwithstanding every appearance of truth, you suppose their testimony to be false, inexplicable circumstances of glaring absurdity crowd upon you. You must suppose that twelve men of mean birth, of no education, living in that humble station which placed ambitious views out of their reach, and far from their thoughts, without any aid from the state, formed the noblest scheme that ever entered into the mind of man, adopted the most daring means of executing that scheme, conducted it with such address as to conceal the imposture under the semblance of simplicity and virtue. You must suppose that men guilty of blasphemy and falsehood, united in an attempt the best contrived—and which has, in fact, proved the most successful—for making the world virtuous. You must also suppose that they formed this singular enterprise without seeking any advantage for themselves, with an avowed contempt of loss and profit, and with the certain expectation of scorn and persecution. In addition, although conscious of one another's villainy, none of them ever thought of providing for his own security by disclosing the fraud, but that amidst the most grievous sufferings to flesh and blood, they persevered in their conspiracy to *cheat* the world into *piety, honesty,* and *benevolence.* Truly those who can swallow such suppositions have no title to object to miracles."

THE SWOON THEORY

Second, there was the "swoon theory" that wasn't thought of until the 1800s by a man named Karl Venturini. The swoon theory says that Jesus simply became unconscious, went into some sort of shock, was placed in the tomb, and there in the cool freshness of the tomb, He revived and walked out and confused the disciples into thinking He had risen from the dead.

It is interesting that from antiquity there is not the slightest suggestion for 1,800 years that Jesus didn't really die. In fact, it was quite certainly the view of the Sanhedrin that Jesus was dead. It was the view of the Praetorium that Jesus was dead. It was the view at Calvary that Jesus was dead. It was the view of the soldiers and the priests and Pilot and the disciples that Jesus was dead.

The theory that the disciples stole the body will not work either. Keep in mind that those who crucified Jesus were in a very unusual business: the business of making people who were alive into people who were dead—and they were experts at what they did.

They not only crucified Christ (which by itself would have killed Him), but before crucifying Him they scourged Him. Then to make absolutely sure that He was dead, they pierced His heart with a Roman spear. John testified that when the spear pierced the pericardium (the sac around the heart) of Christ, there came out water and blood. (Keep in mind that this took place 1,800 years before William Harvey discovered the circulation of blood.) This was simply a layman's way, in that time, to explain the fact that the blood, having gathered in the pericardium, had been there long enough without circulation to have separated; the heavier red corpuscles had settled to the bottom and the clear liquid (which confused John into thinking it was water) was on top. So the fact of the separation of the red corpuscles and the clear liquid is absolute, conclusive medical proof of death.

Jesus was then placed in a tomb, and the swoon theory naively says that in the coolness of the tomb He was resuscitated. If a person is almost dead and going into shock, do you put him in a refrigerator? Of course not. The first thing you do is cover him with blankets to keep him warm lest he go into complete shock and dies. In fact, the coolness of the tomb, doctors will attest, would have been one of the very things that would have certainly killed Him—if Jesus hadn't already been dead, which He was.

But, then, on the third day, having awakened from the refreshing stay in the coolness of the tomb, Jesus stood upon His pierced feet, took His pierced hands and placed them against the inside of a several ton stone, and rolled it aside. He then overpowered sixteen armed Roman guards and went on a seven-mile hike that afternoon on the road to Emmaus, while all of the time preaching to those who were with Him about the predictions in the Old Testament. Having accomplished that, He then struck out for Galilee, almost a hundred miles north, and when He arrived there He climbed a mountain.

It is interesting that these theories were not only

demolished by the church, but also by the critics themselves. For example, the skeptic David Friedrich Strauss, himself no believer in the Resurrection, gave the death-blow to the swoon theory when he wrote:

> [I]t is impossible that a being who had stolen half-dead out of the sepulchre, who crept about weak and ill, wanting medical treatment, who required bandaging, strengthening and indulgence, and who still at last yielded to his sufferings, could have given to the disciples the impression that he was a Conqueror over death and the grave, the Prince of Life, an impression which lay at the bottom of their future ministry. Such a resuscitation could only have weakened the impression which He had made upon them in life and in death, at the most could only have given it an elegiac voice, but could by no possibility have changed their sorrow into enthusiasm, have elevated their reverence into worship.

With Strauss' critique, the swoon theory swooned away.

THE HALLUCINATION THEORY

The third naturalistic theory that was set forth to disprove the Resurrection was the "hallucination theory." According to this theory, the disciples merely thought they saw Jesus; instead they were having visions or hallucinations. Like all of these naturalistic theories, this one is also easily demolished. For example, it is now known and admitted on all sides by experts in this matter that hallucinations are idiosyncratic; they are very personal and individual. You don't have a large group of people having the same hallucination at the same time.

Jesus appeared to three, to eight, to eleven, even to 500 people at one time. The idea that all of these people were having hallucinations is inconceivable. Then, of course, there is Thomas, whom Jesus invited to put his fingers into the nail prints in His hands and to put his hand into the wound in His side. John said, *"That . . . which we have heard, which we have seen with our eyes, which we looked upon and have touched with our hands . . . we proclaim also to you"* (1 John 1:1,3). This was no hallucination off in the dark somewhere, but for forty days Christ appeared to them in every possible circumstance.

THE WRONG TOMB THEORY

The idea has also been set forth that the women went to the wrong tomb. This could be considered part of the fraud theory—sort of a mistake theory. The women went to the wrong tomb, then came back and said that Jesus had risen. Of course, the angel who told them that He was risen must have gone to the wrong tomb also. Then, of course, Peter and John ran also to the wrong tomb, and then they began to proclaim that Jesus had risen from the dead. The Sanhedrin, immediately wanting to check it out, went to the wrong tomb. The Romans then went to the wrong tomb. Everybody went to the wrong tomb—while just a few hundred yards away stands a guard of Roman soldiers who are still keeping guard at the *right* tomb. Of course, none of them ever thought to say: "Hey fellows, we're over here!" Well, that was the wrong theory.

THE LEGENDARY THEORY

Lastly, there was the "legendary theory"—the idea that this whole story just sort of grew up over the first three or four centuries and it's a very late edition. Well, this could possibly have been passed off in the nineteenth century when people were saying the Gospels were written in the third and fourth centuries. But now we know this is not the case. They were all written within the first century and the teaching of the Resurrection goes back almost to the very time that Christ was raised from the dead.

Furthermore, on Pentecost, Peter, in the very first Christian sermon that was preached, preached about the resurrection of Jesus Christ from the dead. In fact, if you analyze Peter's great sermon at Pentecost you will find that if you take out the resurrection from the dead, it not only does great damage to his sermon—it utterly destroys it because he deals with the resurrection of the dead from a number of different directions. If you take out the Resurrection, there is not just a little bit left— there is *nothing* left.

The apostles were chosen as those who were eye wit- nesses of the Resurrection. The message they proclaimed right from that very date in 30 A.D.—as even the skeptical historians now admit—was that Christ had been raised from the dead. It was not some later mythical legendary theory that was added.

Many people say, "We don't know anything about Jesus but what we read in the Bible." People who say that are simply saying, "I am ignorant about the facts of which I speak. I do not know what I am talking about." However, I hope that you will give great credence to what I say because the facts are that in the very first century, from the time that Christ died—in that very first hundred years or so—there are eighteen different pagan unbelieving skeptical writers who write about over one hundred facts concerning the birth, life, ministry, character, miracles, betrayal, trial, conviction, crucifixion, Resurrection and proclamation of Jesus Christ. Virtually the entire history of Christ can be reconstructed by simply using first century pagan authorities.

No, the Resurrection is not mythical or legendary. The interesting thing is that all of the naturalistic schemes were destroyed in the nineteenth century by different critics themselves.

One critic said of the Resurrection, "No, that didn't happen. Here's how I am going to explain it . . ." and he explained it away. A next critic came along and said, "Why, that's ridiculous! Any fool can see the holes in that. Here's how you explain away the Resurrection." Thus, a third theory was advanced and then a fourth, and so they all shot one another down leaving nothing but the Resurrection. So today there is virtually no scholar who would put his reputation on the line by even espousing one of these naturalistic theories.

I recently read the account and the transcript of a debate on the Resurrection. The "con" position against the Resurrection was being taken by a very knowledge-able philosopher, Dr. Antony Flew from England, one of the world's leading atheistic philosophers of his day. He said that we really don't know what happened and he really had no theory to put forth. He said that simply because he knew there is no single possible naturalistic explanation for the resurrection of Christ, he had to appeal to some sort of agnosticism.

OVERWHELMING EVIDENCE

But, my friends, that is not the case. We, in fact, do *know* quite well. The evidence is overwhelming. As I said in the beginning, and as Professor Thomas Arnold said, there is no fact in history that is better proved and supported by more types of evidences than is the resurrection of Jesus Christ from the dead. However, after all I have said, it will still be simply an intellectual concept until you come to know Him personally in the laboratory of your own soul.

Jesus Christ is alive and the ultimate test of that is when you invite Him to walk, not only out of the tomb, but into your heart and to transform the deadness of your life into the glorious resurrection of life He can give: that eternal, never-ending life that only Christ can bestow upon those who will receive Him and trust in Him.

Won't you, if you have never done so, invite Him into your heart today saying, "Come risen Christ, Conqueror of the grave, You died for me." You then will know most assuredly, not only intellectually but also experientially, that Jesus Christ was raised from the dead by the glory of the Father (Romans 6:4) and He is alive because He is alive in you.

PRAYER: *Father, we thank You for the glorious fact of the resurrection of Christ—that we do not follow cunningly devised fables or myths but certainties and facts. We thank You, O Christ, that You died, and You died for us and rose again. Lord, if there are those here who do not know Jesus personally, I pray that You would move them by your Spirit to say, "Come into my heart, Lord Jesus. Come in today; come in to stay." In His name, Amen.*

ABOUT THE AUTHOR

D. James Kennedy, Ph.D. (1930-2007). Because of his internationally syndicated television and radio broadcasts, Dr. Kennedy was the most-listened-to Presbyterian minister in history. For 48 years, he was the senior pastor of Coral Ridge Presbyterian Church in Fort Lauderdale, Florida, where Evangelism Explosion International was launched. Kennedy authored 70 books, including the bestsellers, *Evangelism Explosion*, *Why I Believe*, and (with Dr. Jerry Newcombe) *What If Jesus Had Never Been Born?* He founded Coral Ridge Ministries (now known as D. James Kennedy Ministries), Westminster Academy, and Knox Theological Seminary. In 2005, he was inducted into the National Religious Broadcasters' "Hall of Fame."

The Kennedy Collection also includes
DVD and **CD** sets of these compelling
and passionate messages on the
sanctity of human life.

> **6-DVD set** (720170)
> **6-CD set** (740326)

A Study Guide and **Leader's
Guide** written by a long-time
leader in the pro-life movement,
John Aman, are also available for
use with this unique collection.
These materials make an ideal set
to use with your small group or
Sunday school class.

> **Study Guide** (115955)
> **Leader's Guide** (115956)